Island Treasure:
Florida's Key Deer

Carol Morrison   Nancy Chatelaine

Island Treasure: Florida's Key Deer

Carol Morrison   Nancy Chatelaine

Graphics and photos by Nancy Chatelaine
except where noted.

© Copyright 2017
Palm Frond Press

**PALM FROND PRESS
BIG PINE KEY, FLORIDA USA**
email shadowlane422@gmail.com

Dedication

This book is dedicated to all those who have taken it upon themselves to care about the fate of the Key deer, beginning with cartoonist Ding Darling, Boy Scout Gary Allen and first refuge manager Jack Watson, who saved the Key deer from extinction. Their early efforts have been continued through the decades by too many men and women to name here. The work is both ongoing and infinite. Refuge staff, volunteers, residents, and others interested in protecting our living treasure, work together year after year to ensure the wellbeing of the Key deer. This book is for all of them.

Acknowledgments

Most of the content of this book comes from twenty years experience on this island and a deep-seated interest in the Key deer. Some facts and details are part of interviews with refuge biologists and long time volunteers. Refuge personnel checked our work for accuracy, and local residents shared their stories about the deer.

And, as always, thanks to George and Richie, our husbands, for their support of our work.

Table of Contents

Island Treasure

Foreword

The history of the Florida Keys is filled with tales of adventure, intrigue, and gold. From Spanish explorers to ruthless pirates, a broad array of treasure seekers have been drawn to the Keys, too often exploiting the indigenous peoples and animals. Even today, the ocean continues to reveal long-lost ships with centuries-old cargo and, occasionally, treasure. Venues from Key Largo to Key West offer eager visitors an opportunity to relive those colorful swashbuckling days.

Far away from the shops, souvenirs and pirate regalia, however, hide the *real* Keys treasure: a herd of tiny deer whose existence was imperiled only fifty years ago. These gentle animals have endured hunger, hunters and loss of habitat, and are alive today only because of the eleventh hour intervention of a small group of informed and dedicated people.

Island Treasure

Preface

Dusk in the refuge is magic. As shadows lengthen, night creatures leave their safe daylight havens to find food and water. Most are the usual inhabitants of woodlands: opossums, raccoons and rodents. Other are endangered species, found only here in the National Key Deer Refuge, and dependent upon our pine rocklands and the good will of island residents to keep their species alive. The most prominent among them are the Key deer. Each year thousands of visitors from across the United States and around the world travel to the refuge in order to see for themselves the remarkable Key deer.

The tiny Key deer – about the size of a large dog – are a living study of the persistence of life and its adaptation to the environment. But in the first half of the Twentieth Century, after thousands of years of abundance, the Key deer herd dwindled rapidly from plentiful to endangered; and at one time, not long ago, their very existence was threatened. Only a famous cartoonist, a Boy Scout, a hunting club and a larger-than-life first Refuge Manager saved them from certain extinction. This fortunate conjunction of interest may not have been magic, but it certainly was extraordinary.

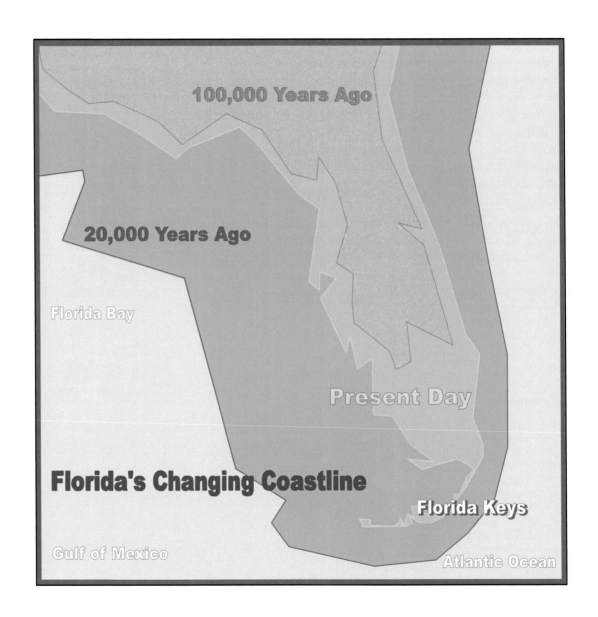

Florida's Changing Coastline

100,000 Years Ago

20,000 Years Ago

Florida Bay

Present Day

Florida Keys

Gulf of Mexico

Atlantic Ocean

How Did the Deer Get Here?

The simple answer is that they've almost always been here. Very slowly, over thousands of years, glaciers grow and shrink, according to cycles of cold or warmth around the globe. As a result, Florida's coastline and land mass has changed dramatically over the eons.

About 100,000 years ago, during a particularly warm time period, all of south Florida was under water. What is now the Keys was a thriving coral reef, with most of it as deep as 30 feet.

Then the planet went through a cooling phase; the glaciers at the poles grew, and as they grew, the water subsided, exposing so much more land that the Florida Peninsula was nearly three times larger. Around 20,000 years ago, there were hills and valleys, lakes and streams, and various animal species, including the Virginia whitetail deer, who inhabited the entire peninsula.

Slowly, the earth began to change again. As the earth warmed, the glaciers melted and the sea level rose, eventually leaving the coastline as it is today. The Key deer were stranded on these islands.

Unfortunately, today, sea levels continue to rise at a rate fast enough to make climate change a critical threat to the deer. Each year more and more deer habitat is lost to the ocean.

We know that the deer were here long before recorded history. The first written sighting was recorded on Columbus' voyage, more than 500 years ago. Other ships' logs mention Key deer as a food source. Interestingly, scant mention is made of the deer again until the 20th century.

A Key deer doe grazes in front of a neighborhood fence. Fences in the Keys are rarely more than four feet tall.

Island Treasure

Why Are the Deer So Small?

The same rising sea levels that formed the Keys also greatly reduced the deer's food supply. The herd was completely isolated on various small islands. Because the food supply was scarce, the smallest individuals were more likely to survive, simply because they needed less food. These were the deer that survived to interbreed. As time passed, the deer became smaller and smaller, resulting in the diminutive subspecies inhabiting the Keys today. Since the environmental and geographical conditions of the Keys are unique, the National Key Deer Refuge is the only place on earth with a herd of these tiny deer.

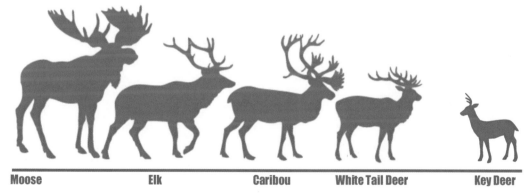

| Moose | Elk | Caribou | White Tail Deer | Key Deer |

The size of the Key deer relative to some of their "cousins".

Looking up at the camera in hopes of a treat. Key deer no longer fear hunting parties, but there are plenty of other threats.

Island Treasure

Twentieth Century Treasure:
Key Deer Return to the Historical Record

Much like pirate treasure, widespread notice of the Key deer lay buried for hundreds of years. Only a few people outside of the Keys knew of the deer's existence, and those who did live in the sparsely populated Keys took the herd's presence for granted. Residents of Key West regarded the deer as their own private hunting stock, located conveniently up the road on Big Pine Key.

The hunting was merciless and unabated. The deer had no place to run. Hunters with big dogs and big guns killed deer indiscriminately. Barbeques, both public and private, featured meat from the tiny deer, with no one questioning the ethics of the hunt or the hunters — until cartoonist J.N. "Ding" Darling aroused public sympathy with a drawing depicting the ugliness of the hunt. A print of his 1934 drawing hangs today in the front hall of the refuge office, and has been reprinted countless times over the years. It is hard to imagine the survival of the Key deer without Darling's graphic depiction of the slaughter.

Surprisingly, despite the temporary public outrage ensuing from Darling's cartoon, written rediscovery of the Key deer did not reappear until the middle of the century. Recalling his visit years earlier, naturalist Robert P. Allen marveled at the "toy deer" of the Florida Keys, in an article he wrote for *Natural History Magazine*, in February 1951.

A few years earlier, in 1947, Allen had taken his young son Gary to see the Florida Keys. Filled with his father's wondrous tales of the "toy deer," Gary wanted to see them for himself. He was so moved by their plight that he

The infamous cartoon that saved a species. Courtesy Ding Darling Society

organized a letter-writing campaign within his Boy Scout troop, sending letters to dignitaries, including Presidents Truman and Eisenhower, to ask that land be set aside to protect the nearly extinct Key deer. Soon, the Boone and Crockett Club put their considerable influence behind the idea of creating a deer refuge. This organization is dedicated to the preservation of wildlife and the ethics of hunting, and people listen when they speak. Both the public and elected officials began to take notice. Three quarters of that "magic" convergence of influence were then in place: the cartoonist, the Boy Scout and the hunting club.

But the hunting continued. By 1950, only twenty-five to thirty deer remained.

The National Key Deer Refuge was established in 1954, but even then, poaching was rampant. Big Pine at that time was still largely unpopulated, with no one empowered to challenge the poachers.

It was time to make magic happen.

The scene was set for a larger-than-life hero, and the man of the moment was already in the Keys: Jack Watson was named the first refuge manager. He was a big man with a big territory and even bigger ideas. He was determined, singlehandedly, to save the Key deer. And he did.

Hunters and their bounty -- Key Deer. Courtesy USFWS

Jack Watson had joined the National Fish and Wildlife Service in 1946, where he was assigned to an area extending from the Tamiami Trail in the Everglades, through the Keys and out to Dry Tortugas. He worked the territory alone and well. He was rough enough to shoot his gun as a warning over the heads of poachers, and gentle enough to teach little children about the refuge. Watson knew the future of the Key deer depended on education.

Under the strong leadership of Jack Watson, the herd grew from only three or four dozen to between 250 and 300. In 1973, the National Wildlife Federation named him Conservationist of the Year, in recognition of his success. Watson retired in 1975, and was followed by a series of refuge managers and wildlife biologists who continue to vigorously protect the tiny deer. At the present time, the size of the herd is estimated to be about 700. Of that number, the great majority are concentrated on Big Pine and No Name Keys, with small numbers on twenty two other, smaller islands in the Lower Keys.

Jack Watson. Courtesy USFWS

Island Treasure

Protecting the Treasure

Research and Observation

With the herd stabilized, opportunities for their study abounded. Over time, the National Key Deer Refuge staff grew from Jack Watson working alone, to a refuge manager, assistant manager and several biologists. Although some biologists — in fact most — at some time study species and issues other than deer, the Key deer remain a primary focus. In a sense, however, all refuge research concerns the deer, since the ecosystem here intricately and permanently connects all forms of wildlife, both flora and fauna.

Refuge staff are not the only professionals who have had a sustained concern about the Key Deer. In the late 1990's, Texas A&M University graduate students conducted an intensive study of the herd. The number of deer deaths had been increasing each year, largely due to an increase in vehicular traffic. Put simply, cars were killing deer at a rate faster than their species could reproduce. The focus, then, was how to protect the deer from dying on the highway.

The students attached radio collars to various does as a means of tracking their movement. One result of this study showed what refuge personnel already knew: most Key deer deaths occur on US1. A high steel fence now borders both sides of the highway on the eastern side of Big Pine. Underpasses run underneath the highway to allow deer a safe passage to the other side. The impact of this measure is still a subject of debate among residents, but cameras have recorded some deer using the passageways. Currently, similar fences and tunnels have been installed in areas of the Everglades where panthers roam: there is an assumption of tangible benefits of wildlife fences and tunnels in south Florida.

Scientific study of the Key deer is ongoing. As time passes, more sophisticated research tools become available. For example, area grids now provide a standardized yet simple means to track many deer, simultaneously, in different parts of the refuge.

Legal Protection

Legal protections of the Key deer are already in place and there are stringent penalties for anyone caught harming or harassing them. Refuge law enforcement personnel are empowered to intervene in any potential threats from humans. While it is hard to believe, some people occasionally swerve their cars to hit the deer. Thankfully, such wanton cruelty is rare, but when it does occur, the full power of the laws falls on the guilty driver.

More often, drivers on both US1 and local roads are ticketed for speeding. Signs warn: Speed Kills Key Deer. The county sheriffs deputies and state law enforcement are very visible and do stop those who violate the law. On US1, the daytime speed limit is forty five mph. The nighttime limit is thirty five.

Refuge law enforcement officers can also cite trespassers who enter posted refuge land. These areas are clearly marked with 'Closed area, do not enter' signs. Since much of the refuge land is open to hikers, there really is no reason for anyone to disregard the law.

The most flagrant offenses, however, are also the most frequent: feeding the Key deer. To do so is a federal crime. Nevertheless, the practice continues, often fueled by internet stories that mislead visitors into thinking that feeding the deer is part of the Key deer experience. It is not. Ever. Feeding the deer causes changes in their behavior that can prove fatal.

As a result of feeding deer from a car or elsewhere, the deer are conditioned to regard cars and people as sources of food. This practice accounts for more Key deer deaths than all the rest combined. Deer run to people and cars for a quick handout, not understanding that most cars

aren't prepared to stop. The result is often another Key deer death. The sad aftermath, a running tally of Key deer deaths throughout the year, is posted at the juncture of Key Deer Blvd. and US1. The numbers prove that the rate of deaths is rising, most of them indirect results of illegal feeding. Key deer can be closely observed in other, legal, ways.

While road deaths remain the single most frequent cause of death, other fatal results of feeding the deer are also significant. The deer's digestive system is not geared to human food. Some dry foods, such as cracked corn, expand inside the stomach and create impactions, some fatal. Other foods such as iceberg lettuce, carry no nutritional value, even though the deer feels full. Recently, communal feeding of Key deer has been found to transfer contagious fatal diseases from one individual to another. The most serious are "lumpy jaw" in which the jaw grows out of alignment until the deer dies from starvation; and a bacterial infection that creates a deadly abscess in the brain. Until recently the brain abscesses were thought to be transmitted from one buck to another during rutting season, when males use their antlers head-on in their battles over females. Now however, some females have developed the disease, very likely as the result of coming into physical contact with one another during communal feedings

There is no good reason to feed Key Deer.

Island Treasure

Maintaining the Treasure

Studying the Deer

Just as old-time pirates sorted through their gold and jewels, again and again, to identify and hold onto their treasure, the National Key Deer Refuge pursues, daily, ways to ensure the well-being of the deer. The status of the herd is always in flux.

Basic Facts about the Deer

Key deer are much smaller than those on the mainland. They are the smallest subspecies of the Virginia white tail. Compared to their northern cousins, Key deer are a little more than half their size. Key deer vary in color from rusty brown to gray, with a dark mask running down their faces. They range from twenty-four to thirty-two inches in height, and sixty-five to eighty-five pounds in weight. Males are bigger than females. Some observers now believe that the deer living in residential neighborhoods seem to be growing bigger than the wild members of the herd, primarily due to feeding by humans and habitual raiding of garbage cans by the deer. In this case, however, bigger is not better. Deer can look well fed and still be malnourished, just as we see in human populations.

The Bucks

The autumn months bring rutting — or mating — season, when males compete for the chance to breed. This practice ensures that genes from the strongest and healthiest males are inherited by the fawns. During rutting season, formerly docile males may become aggressive, even to humans. Residents occasionally tell of encountering a buck during rutting season and being run off the path. After the season, these same bucks will resume their usual gentle nature.

Bucks fight each other with their antlers, sometimes causing visible injury. Many bucks carry significant

scars. Sometimes a buck even loses an antler during a fight — but since deer drop their antlers each spring, loss of an antler is not cause for alarm. Their antlers begin immediately to re-grow, and by August, the bucks' antlers are ready to fight again. When new antlers are grown, they are covered at first with a velvety coating that bucks scrape off against trees. Sometimes a bloody residue remains, and visitors become concerned. There is no cause for worry: this is a normal part of the process. Soon the buck will display the handsome brown antlers we are accustomed to seeing in photos.

The Does and the Fawns

In Key deer, pregnancy lasts about seven months, with most fawns born between April and June. Fawns weigh between two and four pounds at birth. Most does produce only one fawn,

A doe pauses in a driveway to groom her baby.

but it is not unusual to see twins. One resident who lives deep in the woods and sees the same deer every day, reports that one of the does routinely gives birth to twins. Like human mothers, Key deer females keep their fawns close by at first, then gradually allow them more distance, until the young deer is left on his own when the doe is preparing to birth another fawn. Small groups of these newly emancipated deer are not uncommon. Sometimes, well-meaning people see these recently disengaged fawns and mistakenly assume they have been abandoned and are in danger of starving. Not true. The fawns have been taught how and where to forage for food, and nature now insists that they do so.

Man and the Deer

Ensuring the health and safety of the deer, however, is a complex effort, due largely to the presence of man. The deer have been forced out of so much of their habitat that the herd has now reached its optimal level, and cannot support much more growth. Many deer today live alongside humans in small subdivisions scattered across their former territory. Man's presence causes additional dangers beyond the insufficiency of the land to support more deer. Roads crisscross Big Pine and parts of No Name, increasing the chances of deer darting out of the woods in front of cars. Wise drivers are always watching the roadsides for deer; and when one darts across the road, others often follow. Deer do not look both ways before crossing. Again, the misplaced kindness of humans stopping cars to feed the deer increases the danger. Illegal feeding of deer is so rampant that in late afternoon, it is not uncommon to see deer waiting along the roadside for cars to stop, or hiding just inside the tree line, waiting to rush out at the merest sign of food. Some deer are so strongly conditioned to associate cars with food that odd things happen. A Big Pine artist tells how one day he was loading his artwork into his car, when a deer pushed past him and tried to climb into the car, thinking that anything a human puts into a car must be food.

Many residents of the Keys moved here because they love boating, swimming and fishing. To appeal to these buyers, speculators cut networks of canals in some of the subdivisions. Deer don't often drown, but if they fall into a canal at night or unobserved during the day, the result is sad. While deer are excellent swimmers, it is almost impossible for them to climb out of a canal after a fall. Eventually they die of exhaustion. The canal walls are steep and cut deeply enough to leave a margin of about three feet between the water at high tide and the top of the seawall. One refuge biologist recently told of being called three times in two days to rescue the same deer from the same place in the same canal. Just as they fail to look before crossing roads, deer don't always look where they are walking — or remember after an accident. Tiny fawns have been found drowned in mosquito ditches, very shallow ditches cut through the caprock to hold gambusia, tiny fish that eat mosquito larvae. Older deer sometimes trip on the ditches and break a foot or leg. Even man's smallest incursions into deer habitat can prove fatal for the deer.

Fences, nets and even clotheslines pose a threat to Key deer. Not understanding how nets work, the deer sometimes run right into the rope, then twisting and turning to get out, become badly entangled. Homeowners call the refuge to extricate the deer, but on occasion the same deer will run again into the same net or clothesline. Thin wire fences can trap a deer's feet in an

Construction fencing is hazardous to Key deer.

Island Treasure

almost indiscernible opening, and break the deer's foot. It is almost impossible to anticipate and then remove all potential dangers to the deer. Living in a wildlife refuge is very different from living elsewhere, and it carries with it certain responsibilities.

Finally, throughout the refuge, signs warn pet owners to keep their dogs leashed. Free-roaming dogs group together and run deer to death, much like the scene depicted in Ding Darling's drawing. Fortunately, most dog owners recognize the danger and keep their dogs leashed.

The Bright Side

The situation of the Key deer is not entirely bleak. For those of us who live in the refuge, the deer are sometimes funny and often delightful. Deer tend to be territorial and cover the same ground every day, often several times, looking for food. They know where the biggest hibiscus tree is located and compete for its blossoms. They know where the big mango tree grows and stand under it, waiting for fruit to fall. The deer and their routines become so familiar that it is tempting to give them names and treat them as pets. The deer would like nothing better - as long as it results in food. Those big black eyes and gentle demeanor are hard to resist, but anyone who loves the deer *must* resist the impulse to domesticate them. They are wild creatures and need to stay wild if they are to stay alive.

However, that doesn't mean we can't watch them and enjoy the show. Deer are so friendly that they even develop friendships with other species. Just down the street, a neighborhood deer and a cat somehow became friends. Most mornings they just spend time resting together in the front yard of the cat's owner's house. Sometimes they share a bowl of water — but mostly they just share companionship. An even more unusual friendship is currently visible outside a local breakfast spot. At the same time each day, early in the morning, a rooster comes out of the woods and perches on the handle of a shopping cart, and waits. Soon, he is joined by his friend, a Key deer. They walk here and there, enjoying each other's company, until cars begin to fill the parking lot; then they go their separate ways — until the next day, when the same thing happens again.

Why Are Key Deer Still Endangered?

With the deer herd numbering more than any time in refuge records, many observers ask why the Key deer remain on the federal list of endangered species. The answer is easy: They will always be endangered because they are found only in the Lower Keys, where a category IV hurricane would decimate the herd.

Then, why, some ask, doesn't the refuge collect all the deer and spread them across various uninhabited islands? Not only would this action mitigate the loss of deer to deadly hurricanes, it would also solve the problems of people feeding the deer and the loss of deer to vehicles on the road.

Tiny twin fawns almost disappear in the underbrush.

There are many reasons why relocation would not work: Not all uninhabited islands could support deer. Very small islands often do not have an adequate supply of food and water. Indeed, many islands have no permanent fresh water at all. Even though some does swim to the safety of nearby islands to give birth to their fawns, they still must swim back daily to Big Pine or No Name for water. Small islands also would not provide enough edible plant life for the foraging of an ever-growing deer population. Quite simply, the Key deer stay on Big Pine and No Name because they choose to do so. Most efforts to relocate some of the deer to uninhabited islands have been a dismal failure. The deer just swim back to their preferred home.

The refuge, of course, is well aware of the danger of losing the entire herd to one great catastrophe. They have, very slowly and very cautiously, moved small numbers of deer to Summerland, Sugarloaf and Cudjoe Keys. At first, the deer were restricted by a fence to one very large area. When they became completely acclimated to their new home, the fence was removed. The project has been successful thus far, even though the great majority of Key deer will always remain on Big Pine and No Name Keys.

Island Treasure

Sharing the Treasure

Unlike pirates and privateers who hid their treasure and guarded it fiercely, the National Key Deer Refuge seeks to *share* its treasure. As a national wildlife refuge, it has two missions: to protect and maintain wildlife within its borders; and to share with the public some of its wonders. The endangered Key deer are considered a national treasure, and as Jack Watson, the first refuge manager, began to do sixty years ago, the refuge today offers extensive informational and recreational programs to the public.

The most frequently asked question is 'Where can we see the Key Deer?' it's not so much "Where" as "When". Dusk and dawn are the best times to watch for deer. During the heat of the day, the deer hide in the cool protection of the thick brush to rest, then creep out of the shadows as the sun goes down. They are also active at dawn, before the increasing heat of the day pushes them back into the woods. Deer are *crepuscular*, (opposed to nocturnal or diurnal), they prefer the edge of the day and the edge of the woods. This situation does, however, improve the chance of short term visitors seeing some deer during daylight hours.

Early in the morning and late in the afternoon are the best times of day to see deer. Visitors can ask staff at the National Key Deer Refuge Nature Center for currently recommended trails and walks to enjoy the refuge and see the deer.

Island Treasure

A New Threat to the Deer

The holders of a treasure must watch constantly for outside threats. This is as true of living treasures, such as the Key deer, as it is for pirate gold.

For the last two decades, life has been good for the Key deer. They remain on the endangered species list, which protects them from hunting and harassment by humans, and the refuge oversees the health of the herd and ensures its continued presence on the islands.

However, federal regulations cannot protect the deer from disease. In late summer of 2016, those connected with the refuge began to notice a pattern of serious wounds on a suspiciously large percentage of deer. Investigation soon revealed that the ugly wounds were due to screwworms, the maggot stage of the New World screw fly. This parasite had been virtually eradicated in the United States for over fifty years, but now was showing up in the Key deer.

Screw flies lay their eggs, several hundred eggs each, in the flesh around open wounds. Maggots develop, eat their way through the injury and invade live flesh. Since screwworms still afflict animals in central and south America, it is thought that the Keys flies had migrated with products from those areas. But regardless of its source, the screw fly outbreak in the refuge demanded immediate action. Screw flies are deadly if not treated aggressively—which is hard to do with wild deer. The deer, of course, don't realize that people are trying to help them.

Teams of experts from various federal and state agencies, including USDA, FDA, USFWS and FWCC and others, poured into the refuge and organized command posts to locate and treat affected deer. In some cases, deer were tranquilized, their wounds cleaned and anti-parasite medication administered. Terminal deer, however, had to be humanely euthanized.

Groups of local volunteers worked with the refuge in distributing doramectin, a highly successful anti-parasitic medication, to the herd at large. Besides finding the deer once and treating them, the same procedure had to be followed for weeks with the same deer. The medication is effective for only one week, so each deer had to be sprayed with a bit of colored paint to indicate when it had last been treated.

For the entire autumn of 2016, professionals and volunteers came together to save the deer. The outbreak of screwworms was exacerbated by the rutting season, when bucks fight over females and wound each other, leaving a perfect breeding area for screw flies. By the end of rutting season in December, 121 bucks had died, compared to only eleven females. And these are just the deer we know about. Others, in more remote locations, surely died as well. The current estimate is that about thirteen percent of the herd died from screwworm infestations.

Questions remained: What can we do to prevent recurrences? What can we do to prevent screw flies from invading the mainland? For the short run, all animals, both domestic and wild, were inspected at a station in Key Largo, the gateway to and from the Keys. Once the screwworms were eradicated, the station was closed, but will open again if further screwworms are discovered. If the scourge were to reach ranches in mainland Florida, the impact on the food chain would be enormous. For the long run, the refuge is using sterile male screw flies, imported from Panama, to mate with any existing female flies, thus preventing the screw fly life cycle from continuing here. The threat has been managed successfully, but wildlife experts will remain vigilant for the foreseeable future.

Island Treasure

Afterword

It seems fitting that once again a small group of dedicated people has pulled together to save the Key deer from their most recent threat. The refuge, the pubic, and local volunteers rose immediately to a challenge that could have potentially devastated the herd. While it may be true that a living creature can never be absolutely safe, Florida's Key deer are recovering from this latest threat, and thriving under the protective care of their human benefactors.

Postscript

In my work at the National Key Deer Refuges' Visitor Center people often ask, "If there are so many Key deer, why are they still on the Endangered Species List?" "Well," I say, "In the event of a catastrophic hurricane..." "Oh", they invariably respond, nodding knowingly. Neither of us thinking it could ever really happen.

On September 10, 2017 the unthinkable happened. Irma, the worst hurricane ever, struck Big Pine Key and the other Keys. Catastrophic, devastating destruction. Words and photos cannot describe the emotional toll and the loss — houses destroyed, homes ripped apart. The media's images will be with us forever. But before the media, aid workers, and military arrived, before helicopters and generators and chainsaws, there was silence.

The day after the storm in that eerie quiet, little birds appeared. Warblers 'red starts' cheerful, inquisitive. Cardinals. Ground doves. How did these fragile creatures survive the 150+ mph winds and accompanying tornados that flattened the forest?

In that stunned silence the snap of a twig startles me. A Key deer buck appears, he looks around, confused, and begins munching on the newly fallen leaves and berries now blanketing the ground. I recognize him as one of the bucks we treated in last year's screw worm epidemic. He looks up, nods slightly, and goes back to the feast.

Over the next days, another buck and four females carefully pick their way through fallen branches — all regular visitors to our place — and a new one — a fawn. still wearing the remnants of her infant white spots.

The third day after the storm native palms are already sending up new fronds; the brilliant spring green is for me a symbol of nature's renewal.

In the wake of Irma, the loss of property is horrific — homes, businesses, boats, cars, gone and lives changed forever.

Yet there is hope. Rescue workers come in caravans dispensing food, tarps, supplies; emergency workers repair water, sewer, and power lines. The people in these islands are resilient. Some will leave, others will rebuild and become stronger.

The native trees and plants are tough as well. Irma was the worst but certainly not the first storm to wash over this island. Scientists will doubtless study the impact on these habitats for years.

But today, just days after the storm, the birds are returning. A Keys raccoon chitters in the woods. Frogs and snakes and lizards are going about their lives in the new landscape along with the treasured Key deer.

Nancy Chatelaine
Big Pine Key
October 1, 2017

Want to Learn More?

If you would like to learn more about Florida's Key deer, visit the National Key Deer Refuge online or in person.

Made in United States
Orlando, FL
01 August 2022

20424178R00024